{ 18 }

{ 10 }

{ 6 }

{ 36 }

{ 30 }

{ 22 }

SCRUMPTIOUS ACCESSORIES BY YSOLDA

A Scrumptious Palette

Colour has always been an integral part of my design process, but it isn't usually the first step: I'm more accustomed to working from limited colour palettes. So when Jeni from Fyberspates asked if I'd be interested in creating my own palette, I was so excited by the prospect of choosing any colours at all.

The colours I chose make the most of the yarn's sheen, it practically glows, and all of the patterns were designed to take advantage of the yarn's unique qualities. Combining silky luxury and crisp stitch definition, Scrumptious has always been one of my go to yarns, especially for special little projects. The name of the collection comes from a childhood memory, when I was little I was allowed one sweetie (or candy) a week, on Saturdays, and by the time I'd spent all week deciding what to get it tasted much better. Scrumptious itself is a treat, and I hope you'll find these patterns are little treats to indulge yourself with, even the planning should be enjoyable.

3 weights of Scrumptious are featured in the Saturday Treat collection. All 3 are 2 ply yarns with 45% silk and 55% wool put up in 3½oz / 100g skeins.

SCRUMPTIOUS LACE (1093YDS / 1000M)
A fairly heavy laceweight that is both delicate and substantial with enough structure for the simplest projects. The silk content means that more complex lace blocks out very crisply. Available in Treacle Toffee and Wine Gum.

SCRUMPTIOUS 4PLY / SPORT (400YDS / 365M)
A heavy 4ply or sport weight that works well at a wide range of gauges, I love using it for cables and texture patterns that need both good stitch definition and drape. Available in Dandelion & Burdock and Flying Saucer.

SCRUMPTIOUS ARAN (180YDS / 165M)
Unusually smooth and crisp for a yarn on the chunky end of the spectrum I love using this for "macro" lace and it folds and gathers beautifully. Perfect for luxurious, cosy accessories and in colours to cheer up winter: Sugar Mouse and Empire Biscuit.

WINE
GUM

EMPIRE
BISCUIT

DANDELION
& BURDOCK

TREACLE
TOFFEE

FLYING
SAUCER

SUGAR
MOUSE

ABBREVIATIONS

beg	begin(ning)
bind off	aka cast off
C2B [k1, k1]	slip 1 st to cable needle and hold at back, k1, k1 st from the cable needle
C2B[k1, p1]	slip 1 st to cable needle and hold at back, k1, p1 st from the cable needle
C2F[k1, k1]	slip 1 st to cable needle and hold at front, k1, k1 st from the cable needle
C2F[p1, k1]	slip 1 st to cable needle and hold at front, p1, k1 st from the cable needle
C6B[k2, p2, k2]	slip 4 sts to cable needle and hold at back, k2, sl the 2 purl sts from cable needle back to left needle tip and purl them, k2 sts from cable needle
C6F	slip 3 sts to cable needle and hold at front, k3, k3 sts from cable needle
C6B	slip 3 sts to cable needle and hold at back, k3, k3 sts from cable needle
C8F	slip 4 sts to cable needle and hold at front, k4, k4 sts from cable needle

C8B	slip 4 sts to cable needle and hold at back, k4, k4 sts from cable needle
dpn(s)	double pointed needle(s)
inc	increase
k	knit
k2tog	knit 2 tog (a R leaning dec)
kfb	knit in the front and back of same st
m	stitch marker
m1	make 1 - pick up the strand between the needles with L needle tip and knit into this stitch so that it is twisted to increase 1
p	purl
p2tog	purl 2 together
patt	pattern
pm	place marker
rem	remain(ing)
rep	repeat(ing)
rnd(s)	round(s)

RS	right side
sl	slip X st(s) - all sts are slipped one-by-one purlwise with yarn at WS unless otherwise stated
sl1, k2tog, psso	slip 1 st knitwise, knit 2 tog, lift slipped st over st just worked (a L leaning double dec)
slm	slip marker
ssk	slip, slip, knit - sl 2 sts knitwise individually, insert L needle into slipped sts from L to R, k these 2 sts tog (a L leaning dec)
st st	stockinette / stocking stitch
st(s)	stitch(es)
tog	together
w+t	wrap and turn
WS	wrong side
wyib	with yarn in back
wyif	with yarn in front
yo	yarn over
yo2	double yarn over

SUPPORT

Confused about something in one of the patterns, or have a question? The support page on my website contains links to useful resources, tutorials and frequently asked questions: **www.ysolda.com/support**

BARLEY SUGAR

Loosely knit brioche rib in a laceweight yarn is one of my very favourite fabrics, thick, squishy, and warm but incredibly lightweight. The cowl is worked from end to end, beginning and ending with a stockinette tube that is twisted before the ends are grafted together. This half twist is confined to the stockinette section for a simple, interesting detail.

YARN

Scrumptious Lace in Treacle Toffee, one skein.

NEEDLES

US 6 / 4mm 16" / 40cm circular.

US 6 / 4mm 24" / 60cm or longer circular for working magic loop (2 circulars or dpns can also be used but if using dpns sts will need to be arranged onto 2 needles before and after brioche section).

US 7 / 4.5mm straights or circular for working back and forth in rows.

NOTIONS

Stitch marker, scrap yarn.

GAUGE

24 sts and 27 rows = 4" / 10cm in st st in the rnd with smaller needle.

SIZE

Total circumference: 58" / 1.45m. Brioche rib section approx 14½" / 36.25cm wide, st st section approx 6½" / 16cm wide.

NOTES

Slip all sts purlwise.

When working (yo, sl1, k1) in brioche rib, bring the yarn to the front between the needles, sl1 st and bring the yarn to the back over the needles in order to k the next st. The yarn over will cross over the slipped st and will be k tog with this stitch on the following row as if both loops form a single stitch.

DIRECTIONS

Using US 6 / 4mm 16" / 40cm circular needle and scrap yarn, provisionally cast on 80 sts. Switch to main yarn and join rnd, pm to mark beg of rnd.

Work in st st until tube measures 5" / 12.75cm from cast on edge.

Slide sts onto needle tips so that 40 sts are on each tip and the needles are parallel, with the sts at the beginning of the rnd at the front and the tips pointing towards the right. Use larger needle to work across sts as follows: *p1 from back needle, k1 from front needle, rep from * until all sts have been worked.

Continue to work back and forth in rows using the larger needle.

Next row: sl1 wyif, k1, *yo, sl1, k1, rep from * to end.

Next row: sl1 wyif, *k yo and sl st tog, yo, sl1, rep from * to last st, k1.

Rep last row for every row to create brioche rib pattern. Work approx 48" / 122cm in brioche rib.

Next row: sl1 wyif, *k yo and sl st tog, p1, rep from * to last st, k1.

Hold longer US 6 / 4mm needle with tips parallel in right hand and work across row: *p1 onto back needle tip, k1 onto front needle tip, rep from * to end. Set larger needles aside and continue to work in rounds using the magic loop technique. With the bottom edge joined it will take several rounds for the tube to become apparent. If preferred, at the point when there is enough flexibility for stitches to move smoothly around, switch to shorter needle.

Work 5" / 12.75cm in st st.

K20, pull out right needle tip and slide all sts towards left tip. This changes the position of the beginning of the round to create a twist in the scarf when grafted.

FINISHING

Undo provisional cast on and return resulting live sts to spare small circular needle, graft together with live sts from other end of cowl.

Weave in ends and block to measurements.

PEAR DROP

A delicate semi-circular shawl that can be worked in two sizes. The edging, worked first from side to side, features points incorporating the traditional Cat's Eye mesh pattern combined with columns of fagotting; variations on edgings in this style can be found in many traditional Shetland shawls. It begins and ends with longer points, extending the length of the shawl and making it easier to wear as a scarf. Stitches are picked up from the yarn overs along the straight side of the edging and worked into the centre of the shawl. Ever closer rings of concentric decreases create a semi-circle and are highlighted with a simple double yarn over stripe that echoes the patterning on the edging.

YARN

Scrumptious Lace in Wine Gum.

Approximately ¼ skein for small size, ½ skein for large size.

NEEDLES

US 4 / 3.5mm 24" / 60cm or longer circular.

NOTIONS

Stitch markers.

GAUGE

24 sts and 28 rows = 4" / 10 cm in st st, after blocking out well.

SIZE

Small [Large] Upper edge: approx 48[62]" / 122[157]cm; Centre length: 16[21½]" / 41[55]cm. Shown in smaller size.

DIRECTIONS

LOWER EDGE OF SHAWL

Loosely cast on 41 sts; k 1 row. Work in edging pattern from either written directions or charts. Bind off loosely.

EDGING PATTERN

Note - when directed to k across double yarn overs from previous row drop extra loop off needle and work (k1, p1) into the resulting large stitch.

Row 1 (RS): yo, k2tog, (ssk, yo, k2) twice, pm, k9, (k2tog, yo2, ssk) 5 times, k2tog.

Rows 2, 4, 6, 8, 10, 12, 14, 16, 18: k2tog, k to marker, slm, (p2tog, yo, p2) twice, p2.

Row 3: yo, k2tog, (ssk, yo, k2) twice, slm, k7, (k2tog, yo2, ssk) 5 times, k2tog.

Row 5: yo, k2tog, (ssk, yo, k2) twice, slm, k5, (k2tog, yo2, ssk) 5 times, k2tog.

Row 7: yo, k2tog, (ssk, yo, k2) twice, slm, k3, (k2tog, yo2, ssk) 5 times, k2tog.

Row 9: yo, k2tog, (ssk, yo, k2) twice, slm, k1, (k2tog, yo2, ssk) 5 times, k2tog.

Row 11: yo, k2tog, (ssk, yo, k2) twice, slm, k3, (k2tog, yo2, ssk) 4 times, k2tog.

Row 13: yo, k2tog, (ssk, yo, k2) twice, slm, k5, (k2tog, yo2, ssk) 3 times, k2tog.

Row 15: yo, k2tog, (ssk, yo, k2) twice, slm, k7, (k2tog, yo2, ssk) twice, k2tog.

Row 17: yo, k2tog, (ssk, yo, k2) twice, slm, k9, (k2tog, yo2, ssk) once, k2tog.

Row 19: yo, k2tog, (ssk, yo, k2) twice, slm, k to end.

Work rows 20-39 from * to * a total of 17[26] times.

*Row 20, 22, 24, 26, 28, 30: k to marker, slm, (p2tog, yo, p2) twice, p2.

Row 21: yo, k2tog, (ssk, yo, k2) twice, slm, k9, k2tog, yo2, k2.

Row 23: yo, k2tog, (ssk, yo, k2) twice, slm, k7, k2tog, yo2, ssk, k2tog, yo2, kfb.

Row 25: yo, k2tog, (ssk, yo, k2) twice, slm, k5, (k2tog, yo2, ssk) twice, k2tog, yo2, kfb.

Row 27: yo, k2tog, (ssk, yo, k2) twice, slm, k3, (k2tog, yo2, ssk) 3 times, k2tog, yo2, kfb.

Row 29: yo, k2tog, (ssk, yo, k2) twice, slm, k1, (k2tog, yo2, ssk) 5 times.

Row 31: yo, k2tog, (ssk, yo, k2) twice, slm, k3, (k2tog, yo2, ssk) 4 times, k2tog.

Rows 32, 34, 36, 38: k2tog, k to marker, slm, (p2tog, yo, p2) twice, p2.

Row 33: yo, k2tog, (ssk, yo, k2) twice, slm, k5, (k2tog, yo2, ssk) 3 times, k2tog.

Row 35: yo, k2tog, (ssk, yo, k2) twice, slm, k7, (k2tog, yo2, ssk) twice, k2tog.

Row 37: yo, k2tog, (ssk, yo, k2) twice, slm, k9, k2tog, yo2, ssk, k2tog.

Row 39: yo, k2tog, (ssk, yo, k2) twice, slm, k to end.*

Rows 40, 42, 44, 46, 48, 50, 52, 54, 56: k to marker, slm, (p2tog, yo, p2) twice, p2.

Row 41: yo, k2tog, (ssk, yo, k2) twice, slm, k9, k2tog, yo2, k1.

Row 43: yo, k2tog, (ssk, yo, k2) twice, slm, k7, k2tog, yo2, ssk, k2tog, yo2, kfb.

Row 45: yo, k2tog, (ssk, yo, k2) twice, slm, k5, (k2tog, yo2, ssk) twice, k2tog, yo2, kfb.

Row 47: yo, k2tog, (ssk, yo, k2) twice, slm, k3, (k2tog, yo2, ssk) 3 times, k2tog, yo2, kfb.

Row 49: yo, k2tog, (ssk, yo, k2) twice, slm, k1, (k2tog, yo2, ssk) 4 times, k2tog, yo2, kfb.

Row 51: yo, k2tog, (ssk, yo, k2) twice, slm, k3, (k2tog, yo2, ssk) 4 times, k2tog, yo2, kfb.

Row 53: yo, k2tog, (ssk, yo, k2) twice, slm, k5, (k2tog, yo2, ssk) 4 times, k2tog, yo2, kfb.

Row 55: yo, k2tog, (ssk, yo, k2) twice, slm, k7, (k2tog, yo2, ssk) 4 times, k2tog, yo2, kfb.

Row 57: yo, k2tog, (ssk, yo, k2) twice, slm, k9, (k2tog, yo2, ssk) 4 times, k2tog, yo2, kfb.

Row 58: k to marker, slm, (p2tog, yo, p2) twice, p2.

Bind off loosely.

CENTRE OF SHAWL

When directed to work in st st work a 3 st garter st selvedge by kitting the first and last 3 sts of every row.

Double YO Stripe:

Row 1 (WS): k.

Row 2: k3, (ssk, yo2, k2tog) to 3 sts from end, k3.

Row 3: k, working k1, p1 into double yarn overs as for edging.

PICKING UP STITCHES FROM EDGING

Beginning at cast on edge with RS facing pick up and knit 190[280] sts along straight side of edging, picking up and knitting one stitch into each yo and one loop from corners of cast on and bind off edges.

Large shawl only:

Work 31 rows in st st beg with a p row.

Next row (RS): k6, (k2tog, k1) to 4 sts from end, k4. 190 sts.

Work rows 1-3 of Double YO Stripe once.

DIRECTIONS, CONTINUED

Both sizes:

Work 15 rows in st st beg with a p row.

Next row (RS): k6, (k2tog, k1) to 4 sts from end, k4. 130 sts.

Work rows 1-3 of Double YO Stripe once.

Work 10 rows in st st beg with a k row.

Next row (RS): k6, (k2tog, k1) to 4 sts from end, k4. 90 sts.

Work rows 1-3 of Double YO Stripe once.

Work 6 rows in st st beg with a k row.

Next row (RS): k4, (k2tog, k1) to 2 sts from end, k2. 62 sts.

Work rows 1-3 of Double YO Stripe once.

Work 10 rows in st st beg with a k row.

Next row (RS): k3, k2tog to 3 sts from end, k3. 34 sts.

Work 5 rows in st st beg with a p row.

Next row (RS): k3, k2tog to 3 sts from end, k3. 20 sts.

Work 3 rows in st st beg with a p row.

Next row (RS): k3, k2tog to 3 sts from end, k3. 13 sts.

Next row: k3, p to 3 sts from end, k3.

Next row: k2tog to 1 st from end, k1. 7 sts.

FINISHING

Break yarn and draw through rem sts, pulling up tightly. Weave in ends and block in a semi-circle to match measurements, stretching to open up lace and pinning out points of edging.

KEY

EDGING PATTERN

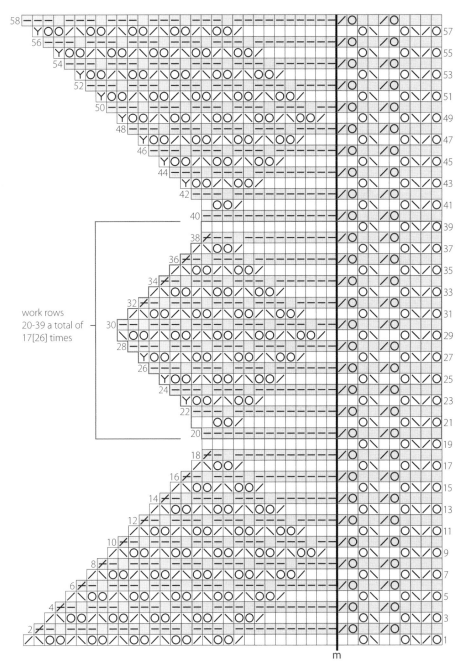

work rows
20-39 a total of
17[26] times

WALNUT WHIP

A cute pixie hat featuring a simple pattern of wide braided cables, Walnut Whip's simplicity doesn't mean there aren't interesting details. Pleating at the back creates a neatly controlled slouchiness that's hidden within the cables: as the other columns on the round are cabled the three pleated sections are pleated in a way that mimics the cabling but pulls the fabric together vertically. Stitches are picked up from the wrong side, several rows below the current round, and are knit together with the live stitches on the needles, the technique is a little awkward but easy to do. Decreases are worked into the cable pattern so that they come together in a point. The silk blend allows patterning like this to be done in such a dark colour, reflecting light to create strong contrast between the prominent and recessed areas of the cables.

YARN

Scrumptious 4 Ply / Sport in Dandelion & Burdock, one skein.

NEEDLES

US 3 / 3mm 16" / 40cm circular needles.

US 4 / 3.5mm 16" / 40cm circular needles.

US 4 / 3.5mm dpns or long circular for preferred method of working small circumferences in the rnd.

NOTIONS

Stich markers, cable needle, scrap yarn.

GAUGE

24 sts and 32 rnds = 4" / 10 cm in st st in the rnd with larger needle.

SIZES

s[m, l] to fit head circumference of approx 19[21, 24]" / 48[53, 61]cm.

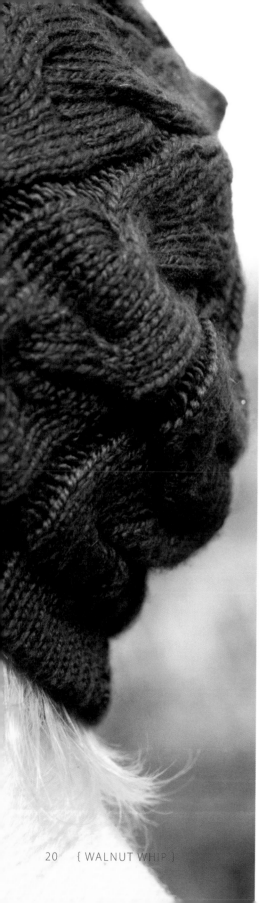

DIRECTIONS

Provisionally cast on 110[121,132] sts. Join working yarn and k 1 row without joining.

Join to work in the rnd being careful not to twist and pm to mark beg of rnd.

Next 19 rnds: (p2, k9) to end.

Undo provisional cast on and slip resulting live sts onto smaller needle. Fold hem in half so that cast on edge is on the inside level with the working stitches and the 2 needles are parallel. Work 1 rnd in (p2, k9) pattern working each working st tog with 1 cast on st as either a k2tog or p2tog.

Next rnd: *p2, k2, (m1, k3) twice, m1, k1, rep from * to end. 140[154, 168] sts.

Next rnd: (p2, C8B, k4) to end.

**Next 9 rnds: (p2, k12) to end.

Next rnd: *p2, k4, using cable needle pick up 4 sts from wrong side level with previous cable rnd directly below the last 4 sts of this 12 st rib; hold cable needle parallel behind working needle and k these 4 sts tog with next 4 working sts, k4, rep from * twice more, (p2, k4, C8F) to end.

Next 9 rnds: (p2, k12) to end.

Next rnd: *p2, k4, using cable needle pick up 4 sts from wrong side level with previous cable rnd directly below the first 4 sts of this 12 st rib, hold cable needle parallel behind working needle and k these 4 sts tog with next 4 working sts, k4, rep from * twice more, (p2, C8B, k4) to end.

Rep from ** once more.

Next rnd: (p2, k12) to end.

Next rnd: *p2, (k2, k2tog) 3 times, rep from * to end. 110[121, 132] sts.

Switch to dpns or other needle for your preferred method of working small circumferences in the rnd.

Next 3 rnds: (p2, k9) to end.

Next rnd: (p2, k5, ssk, k2) to end. 100[110, 120] sts.

Next rnd: (p2, k5, ssk, k1) to end. 90[99, 108] sts.

Next rnd: (p2, k5, ssk) to end. 80[88, 96] sts.

Next 3 rnds: (p2, k6) to end.

Next rnd: (p2, k1, k2tog, k3) to end. 70[77, 84] sts.

Next rnd: (p2, k2tog, k3) to end. 60[66, 72] sts.

Next rnd: (p2tog, k4) to end. 50[55, 60] sts.

Next rnd: (p1, k2, ssk) to end. 40[44, 48] sts.

Next rnd: (k2tog, k2) to end. 30[33, 36] sts.

Next rnd: (k10[11, 12] sts, pm) 3 times.

Next rnd: *k to 2 sts before m, k2tog, slm, rep from * twice more.

Rep last rnd until only 6 sts rem. K2tog around removing markers as you come to them.

FINISHING

Break yarn and draw through 3 rem sts, pulling up tightly and weaving in end on inside. Weave in remaining ends and block.

Sherbet Lemon

Long fingerless mitts featuring a geometric cable pattern: a variation on a traditional pattern of tessellated diamonds arranged so their outlines form a flowing lattice. This pattern takes advantage of the crisp stitch definition of the yarn and the light reflecting silk emphasises the strong relief effect and different textures between the sections worked in reverse stockinette and garter stitch. As the elements of the pattern can be easily scaled the thumb shaping is incorporated within the pattern. The allover cuff pattern flows into a single motif on the back of the hand with a co-ordinating rib pattern on the palms and thumb. Simple decreases incorporated into the stitch pattern create the shaped edge on the cuff.

YARN

Scrumptious 4 ply / sport in Flying Saucer, one skein.

NEEDLES

US 2½ / 3mm dpns or long circular for preferred method of working small circumferences in the rnd.

NOTIONS

Stitch markers, scrap yarn.

GAUGE

30 sts and 38 rows = 4" / 10cm in st st in the rnd.

SIZE

To fit approx measurement around knuckles of 7" / 17.5cm - 8½" / 21.25cm with 0 - 1½" / 3.75cm of negative ease.

When blocked and slightly stretched the length of the mitts is 10¾" / 26cm, and the width across the back of the hand is 3½" / 9cm.

CUFF PATTERN

Rnd 1: k1, p5, k1, p2, k1, p5, k1, p2.

Rnd 2: ssk, k5, p2, k5, k2tog, p2.

Rnd 3: (k1, p4, k1, p2) twice.

Rnd 4: ssk, k4, p2, k4, k2tog, p2.

Rnd 5: (k1, p3, k1, p2) twice.

Rnd 6: C2F[p1, k1], k3, p2, k3, C2B[k1, p1], p2.

Rnd 7: p1, k1, (p2, k1) 3 times, p3.

Rnd 8: p1, C2F[p1, k1], k2, p2, k2, C2B[k1, p1], p3.

Rnd 9: (p2, k1, p1, k1) twice, p4.

Rnd 10: p2, C2F[p1, k1], k1, p2, k1, C2B[k1, p1], p4.

Rnd 11: p3, k2, p2, k2, p5.

Rnd 12: p3, C6B[k2, p2, k2], p5.

Rnd 13: rep rnd 11.

Rnd 14: p2, C2B[k1, k1], k1, p2, k1, C2F[k1, k1], p4.

Rnd 15: p2, k1, p1, k1, p2, k1, p1, k1, p4.

Rnd 16: p1, C2B[k1, k1], k2, p2, k2, C2F[k1, k1], p3.

Rnd 17: p1, k1, (p2, k1) 3 times, p3.

Rnd 18: C2B[k1, k1], k3, p2, k3, C2F[k1, k1], p2.

Rnd 19: k1, p3, k1, p2, k1, p3, k1, p2.

Rnd 20: (k5, p2) twice.

Rnd 21: rep rnd 19.

Rnd 22: k3, C2B[k1, p1], p2, C2F[p1, k1], k3, p2.

Rnd 23: k1, p2, k1, p4, (k1, p2) twice.

Rnd 24: k2, C2B[k1, p1], p4, C2F[p1, k1], k2, p2.

Rnd 25: k1, p1, k1, p6, k1, p1, k1, p2.

Rnd 26: k1, C2B[k1, p1], p6, C2F[p1, k1], k1, p2.

Rnd 27: k2, p8, k2, p2. Stop 4 sts from end of rnd, this will be the new beg of the rnd.

Rnd 28: C6F[k2, p2, k2], p8.

Work first 4 sts of next rnd: k2, p2, then return beg of rnd to this original placement and continue.

Rnd 29: k2, p8, k2, p2.

Rnd 30: k1, C2F[k1, k1], p6, C2B[k1, k1], k1, p2.

Rnd 31: k1, p1, k1, p6, k1, p1, k1, p2.

Rnd 32: k2, C2F[k1, k1], p4, C2B[k1, k1], k2, p2.

Rnd 33: k1, p2, k1, p4, k1, p2, k1, p2.

Rnd 34: k3, C2F[k1, k1], p2, C2B[k1, k1], k3, p2.

Rnd 35: k1, p3, k1, p2, k1, p3, k1, p2.

Rnd 36: (k5, p2) twice.

Rnds 37-51: work rnds 5-19 once more.

KEY

☐ k

⊟ p

⧄ k2tog

⧅ ssk

☐ repeat

⧄⧅ C2B[k1, p1]

⧅⧄ C2F[p1, k1]

⧄⧄ C2B[k1, k1]

⧅⧅ C2F[k1, k1]

⧄⧅ C6B[k2, p2, k2]

⧅⧄ C6F[k2, p2, k2]

NOTES

a. rnds 37-51: work rows 5-19 once more

b. stop 4 sts from end of rnd, this will be the new beg of the rnd

c. work first 4 sts of rnd 29, reposition beg of rnd to this point

CUFF PATTERN

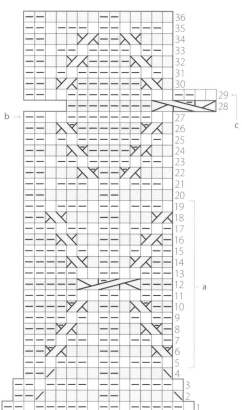

BACK OF HAND PATTERN

Rnd 1: k4, m1, k1, p2, k1, m1, k4.

Rnd 2: k1, p4, k1, p2, k1, p4, k1.

Rnd 3: k5, m1, k1, p2, k1, m1, k5.

Rnd 4: k1, p5, k1, p2, k1, p5, k1.

Rnd 5: k6, m1, k1, p2, k1, m1, k6.

Rnd 6: k1, p6, k1, p2, k1, p6, k1.

Rnd 7: k8, p2, k8.

Rnd 8: rep rnd 6.

Rnd 9: C2F[p1, k1], k6, p2, k6, C2B[k1, p1].

Rnd 10: p1, k1, p5, k1, p2, k1, p5, k1, p1.

Rnd 11: p1, C2F[p1, k1], k5, p2, k5, C2B[k1, p1], p1.

Rnd 12: p2, k1, p4, k1, p2, k1, p4, k1, p2.

Rnd 13: p2, C2F[p1, k1], k4, p2, k4, C2B[k1, p1], p2.

Rnd 14: (p3, k1) twice, p2, (k1, p3) twice.

Rnd 15: p3, C2F[p1, k1], k3, p2, k3, C2B[k1, p1], p3.

Rnd 16: p4, (k1, p2) 3 times, k1, p4.

Rnd 17: p4, C2F[p1, k1], k2, p2, k2, C2B[k1, p1], p4.

Rnd 18: p5, k1, p1, k1, p2, k1, p1, k1, p5.

Rnd 19: p5, C2F[p1, k1], k1, p2, k1, C2B[p1, k1], p5.

Rnd 20: p6, k2, p2, k2, p6.

Rnd 21: p6, C6F[k2, p2, k2], p6.

Rnd 22: rep rnd 20.

Rnd 23: p5, C2B[k1, k1], k1, p2, k1, C2F[k1, k], p5.

Rnd 24: p5, k1, p1, k1, p2, k1, p1, k1, p5.

Rnd 25: p4, C2B[k1, k1], k2, p2, k2, C2F[k1, k1], p4.

Rnd 26: p4, k1, (p2, k1) three times, p4.

Rnd 27: p3, C2B[k1, k1], k3, p2, k3, C2F[k1, k1], p3.

Rnd 28: (p3, k1) twice, p2, (k1, p3) twice.

Rnd 29: p2, C2B[k1, k1], k4, p2, k4, C2F[k1, k1], p2.

Rnd 30: p2, k1, p4, k1, p2, k1, p4, k1, p2.

Rnd 31: p1, C2B[k1, k1], k5, p2, k5, C2F[k1, k1], p1.

Rnd 32: p1, k1, p5, k1, p2, k1, p5, k1, p1.

Rnd 33: C2B[k1, k1], k6, p2, k6, C2F[k1, k1].

Rnd 34: k1, p6, k1, p2, k1, p6, k1.

Rnd 35: k8, p2, k8.

Rnd 36: rep rnd 34.

Rnd 37: k6, C2B[k1, p1], p2, C2F[p1, k1], k6.

Rnd 38: k1, p5, k1, p4, k1, p5, k1.

Rnd 39: k5, C2B[k1, p1], p4, C2F[p1, k1], k5.

Rnd 40: k1, p4, k1, p6, k1, p4, k1.

Rnd 41: k4, C2B[k1, p1], p6, C2F[p1, k1], k4.

Rnd 42: k1, p3, k1, p8, k1, p3, k1.

Rnd 43: k3, C2B[k1, p1], p8, C2F[p1, k1], k3.

Rnd 44: k1, p2, k1, p10, k1, p2, k1.

Rnd 45: k2, C2B[k1, p1], p10, C2F[p1, k1], k2.

Rnd 46: k1, p1, k1, p12, k1, p1, k1.

Rnd 47: k1, C2B[k1, p1], p12, C2F[p1, k1], k1.

Rnd 48: k2, p14, k2.

Rnd 49: k2tog, p14, ssk.

BACK OF HAND PATTERN

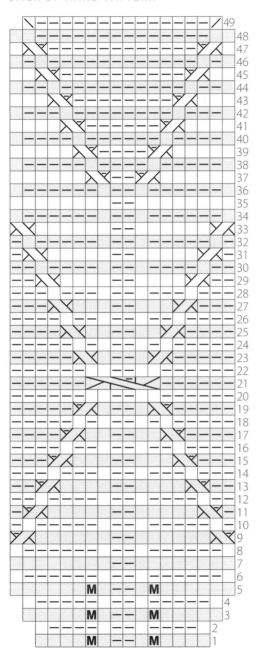

☐ k

⊟ p

◿ k2tog

◺ ssk

M make one

▱◿ C2B[k1, p1]

◺▱ C2F[p1, k1]

▱◿ C2B[k1, k1]

◺▱ C2F[k1, k1]

◺▱◿ C6B[k2, p2, k2]

◺▱◿ C6F[k2, p2, k2]

DIRECTIONS

Cast on 72 sts and join rnd. Divide sts evenly over 4 dpns or in 2 sections for magic loop or 2 circulars.

Rnd 1: (k7, p2) to end.

Rnd 2: (p2, k1, p5, k1) to end.

Rep last 2 rnds twice more, followed by rnd 1 once more.

Following either chart or written directions work 51 rnds in cuff pattern, working 4 repeats of patt on each rnd. 56 sts.

Next rnd: k5, p2, pm, work next 12 sts in back of hand pattern, pm, (p2, k5) to 2 sts from end, p2.

Next rnd: k1, p3, k1, p2, slm, work in back of hand pattern to m, slm, (p2, k1, p3, k1) to 2 sts from end, p2.

Next rnd: k5, p2, slm, work in back of hand pattern to m, slm, (p2, k5) to 2 sts from end, p2.

Rep last 2 rnds 16 more times, ending with rnd 35 of back of hand pattern. 62 sts.

Right mitt only:
Next rnd: work in patt to 2nd m, slm, p2, k1, p3, k1, p1, slip next 14 sts to scrap yarn, cast on 14 sts next to sts just worked and work in patt to end of rnd.

Left mitt only:
Next rnd: work in patt to 15 sts from end of rnd, slip next 14 sts to scrap yarn, cast on 14 sts next to sts just worked, p1.

BOTH MITTS
Continue in patt, incorporating cast on sts into existing garter rib pattern, until back of hand pattern is complete. 60 sts. Bind off.

THUMBS

Remove scrap yarn and slip held sts for thumb onto needle. Join yarn and pick up and k 14 sts from cast on sts for thumb. Divide these 28 sts evenly over needles and join rnd.

Rnd 1: (p1, k1, p3, k1, p1) to end.

Rnd 2: (p1, k5, p1) to end.

Rep these 2 rnds 3 more times, followed by rnd 1 once more.

Bind off.

FINISHING

Weave in ends and block.

EDINBURGH ROCK

I love the classic garter stitch "bow-tie" scarf, an idea that's both adorably cute and practical. There's also something pleasingly knitterly about the construction of the ribbed loop. But, of course, that design already exists and numerous patterns can be found. Rather than totally re-inventing the wheel, Edinburgh Rock is my take on that idea, lengthened to wrap twice around the neck (Scotland is not the place for draughty neckwear!) and with a few additions. The scarf section features columns of simple lace that add interest and create structural folds, and the bow or leaf shape of the ends is echoed in the little leaf motifs. Both leaves are worked down from the ribbed section for perfect symmetry. A slipped stitch, I-cord like, selvedge neatens the edges.

YARN

Scrumptious Aran in Sugar Mouse, two skeins.

NEEDLES

US 8 / 5mm 24" / 60cm circular.

US 8 / 5mm dpn.

NOTIONS

Stitch markers.

GAUGE

18 sts and 26 rows = 4" / 10cm in st st.

SIZE

One size, the finished length of the scarf is 60" / 150cm. The width of the garter stitch section is 5½" / 13.75cm.

NOTES

Slip all sts purlwise with yarn at WS.

DIRECTIONS

RIBBED TAB

Cast on 17 sts.

Row 1 (RS): sl2, (p1, k1) to last st, k1.

Row 2: sl2, (k1, p1) to last st, p1.

Rep last 2 rows 7 more times.

Next row (RS): sl2, kfb 13 times, k2. 30 sts

NECK

Next row (WS): sl2, k5, p5, k6, p5, k5, p2

Next row: sl2, k5, *k2tog, yo, k1, yo, ssk, k6, rep from * once more, k1.

Rep last 2 rows until scarf measures 36" / 91.5cm from top of ribbed tab. Work WS row once more.

RIBBED LOOP

Divide sts onto two needles for front and back of loop: sl 2 sts onto right needle tip, *sl next st onto dpn and hold at back of work, slip next st onto right needle tip, rep from * until 2 sts remain on left needle, slip these 2 sts to the right needle tip.

Ignore the 13 sts held on dpn at back of work while working the 17 sts for the front of the loop.

Next row (RS): sl2, (p1, k1) to last st, k1.

Next row: sl2, (k1, p1) to last st, p1.

Rep last 2 rows 7 more times. Break yarn.

Rejoin yarn and work held sts on dpn with empty working needle. Leave front sts just worked on other needle while working the back of the loop.

Next row (RS): (k1, p1) to last st, k1.

Next row: (p1, k1) to last st, p1.

Rep last 2 rows 7 more times.

Return sts to a single needle by holding the front and back needles parallel in the left hand and working across them with the empty working needle as follows: sl2 sts from front needle, *k1 from front needle, k1 from back, rep from *12 more times, k rem 2 sts from front needle.

Continue to work leaf on these 30 sts.

LEAF

Row 1 (WS): sl2, k to 2 sts from end, p2.

Row 2: sl2, k to end.

Rows 3 - 30: rep last 2 rows 14 more times.

Row 31: rep row 1.

Row 32 (RS): sl2, k17, m1, k1, m1, k10. 32 sts.

Row 33: sl2, k8, p3, k to 2 sts from end, p2.

Row 34: sl2, k16, k2tog, yo, k1, yo, ssk, k to end.

Row 35: sl2, k7, p5, k 2 sts from end, p2.

Row 36: sl2, k15, k2tog, k1, yo, k1, yo, k1, ssk, k to end.

Row 37: sl2, k6, p7, k to 2 sts from end, p2.

Row 38: sl2, k14, k2tog, k2, yo, k1, yo, k2, ssk, k to end.

Row 39: sl2, k5, p9, k to 2 sts from end, p2.

Row 40: sl2, k13, k2tog, k7, ssk, k to end. 30 sts.

Row 41: sl2, k4, p9, k to 2 sts from end, p2.

Row 42: sl2, k12, k2tog, k7, ssk, k to end. 28 sts.

Row 43: sl2, k3, p9, k to 2 sts from end, p2.

Row 44: sl2, k11, k2tog, k7, ssk, k to end. 26 sts.

Row 45: sl2, k2, p9, k to 2 sts from end, p2.

Row 46: sl2, k11, ssk, k5, k2tog, k to end. 24 sts.

Row 47: sl2, k2, p7, k to 2 sts from end, p2.

Row 48: sl2, k11, ssk, k3, k2tog, k to end. 22 sts.

Row 49: sl2, k2, p5. k to 2 sts from end, p2.

Row 50: sl2, k11, ssk, k1, k2tog, k to end. 20 sts.

Row 51: sl2, k2, p3, k to 2 sts from end, p2.

Row 52: sl2, k11, sl1, k2tog, psso, k to end. 18 sts.

Row 53: sl2, k to 2 sts from end, p2

Row 54: sl2, ssk, k to last 4 sts, k2tog, k2. 16 sts.

Rows 55-67: rep rows 53-54 5 more times, then row 53 once more. 6 sts.

Row 68: sl1, ssk, k2tog, k1. 4 sts.

Row 69: sl1, k2, p1.

Row 70: sl1, k2tog, k1. 3 sts.

Break yarn leaving a 6" / 15cm tail, thread through remaining sts and pull tight.

2ND LEAF

With RS facing pick up and k 17 sts across cast on edge of ribbed tab.

Next row (WS): sl2, (k1, p1) to last st, p1

Next row (RS): sl2, kfb 13 times, k2. 30 sts

Work leaf section on these 30 sts as above.

FINISHING

Weave in ends, block to measurements.

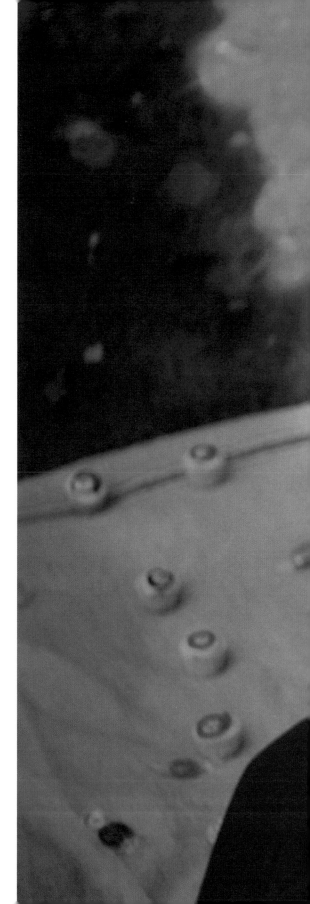

ALMOND COMFIT

Almond Comfit features an unusual construction that has more in common with many shawl patterns than hats. Beginning at the centre of the leaf motif at the front, and increasing within this pattern from just a few stitches to the full width from side edge to edge, the hat is worked from front to back. Reverse stockinette I-cord gives a neat, sturdy edge. Only one row of I-cord is worked for every 2 rows of the hat so it pulls in the edge without the need for any more complex shaping such as short rows. Closely worked decreases at the back create a slightly slouchy, gathered effect; the hat is completed by grafting together the few remaining stitches.

YARN

Scrumptious Aran in Empire Biscuit, one skein.

NEEDLES

US 8 / 5mm 24" / 60cm or longer circular.

SIZE

Finished circumference of approx 19[21, 23]" / 48[53, 58]cm. Shown with zero ease. Choose a size with some negative ease for a closer, less slouchy, fit.

GAUGE

16 sts and 24 rows = 4" / 10cm in st st.

NOTES

Slip all sts purlwise with yarn at wrong side (yarn in back when working RS rows and yarn in front when working WS rows).

Hat will be worked back and forth in rows. For the first few rows, the cast on will pull the bottom edges together. It may be necessary to work across half the stitches, then pull the right needle tip out to slide the sts just worked back onto the cable, and proceed to work the second half of the sts.

DIRECTIONS

CENTER FRONT

Using figure-of-8 method, cast on 12 sts total, 6 on each needle. K6, turn.

Row 1 (RS): sl5 wyib, k1, yo, k1, p5.

Row 2: sl5 wyif, p3, k5.

Row 3: sl5 wyib, k1, yo, k1, yo, k1, p5.

Row 4: sl5 wyif, p5, k5.

Continue working 5 selvedge sts on either side as established - slip the first 5 sts of each row; purl the last 5 on RS rows and knit the last 5 on WS rows.

Begin working sts in between selvedge sts from leaf motif pattern, following either chart or written directions. Purl all WS sts between these selvedge sts. Continue in this manner until all rows of leaf motif have been completed, ending with a WS row. 51 sts.

MAIN BODY OF HAT

Next row (RS): sl5 wyib, k1, yo, k to 6 sts from end, yo, k1, p5. 53 sts.

Next row (WS): sl5 wyif, p to 5 sts from end, k5.

Rep last 2 rows 6[9, 12] more times. 65[71, 77] sts.

*Next row (RS): sl5 wyib, k1, yo, ssk, k to 8 sts from end, k2tog, yo, k1, p5.

Next row (WS): sl5 wyif, p to 5 sts from end, k5. *

Rep last 2 rows from * to * 12[14, 16] more times.

DECREASES AT BACK OF HAT

Next row: sl5 wyib, k1, yo, ssk, (k1, k2tog) to 9 sts from end, k1, k2tog, yo, k1, p5. 49[53, 57] sts.

Work 3 rows in patt as established from * to * above.

Next row: sl5 wyib, k1, yo, ssk, k2tog to 9 sts from end, k1, k2tog, yo, k1, p5. 33[35, 37] sts.

Rep last 4 rows once more. 25[26, 27] sts.

Work 1 row in patt.

Next row: sl5 wyib, k1, yo, ssk, k1[0, 1], (k2tog) to 6 sts from end, yo, k1, p5. 21[21, 22]sts.

Next row (WS): sl5 wyif, p2tog 5[5, 6] times, p1[1, 0], k5. 16 sts.

Next row: sl5 wyib, k2tog 4 times, p3. 12 sts.

FINISHING

Arrange sts so 6 are on each needle tip, hold tips parallel and kitchener st together in patt.

STITCH GUIDE

LEAF MOTIF

Row 1 (RS): k1, (yo, k1) 4 times.

Row 3: (k1, yo) twice, k2, yo, k1, yo, k2, (yo, k1) twice.

Row 5: *k2, yo, k1, yo, k2, rep from * twice more.

Row 7: *k3, yo, k1, yo, k3, rep from * twice more.

Row 9: *k4, yo, k1, yo, k4, rep from * twice more.

Row 11: k1, yo, ssk, k5, k2tog, yo, k1, yo, ssk, k7, k2tog, yo, k1, yo, ssk, k5, k2tog, yo, k1.

Row 13: (k1, yo) twice, ssk, k3, k2tog, yo, k3, yo, ssk, k5, k2tog, yo, k3, yo, ssk, k3, k2tog, (yo, k1) twice.

Row 15: k1, yo, k3, yo, ssk, k1, k2tog, yo, k5, yo, ssk, k3, k2tog, yo, k5, yo, ssk, k1, k2tog, yo, k3, yo, k1.

Row 17: k1, yo, k5, yo, sl1, k2tog, psso, yo, k7, yo, ssk, k1, k2tog, yo, k7, yo, sl1, k2tog, psso, yo, k5, yo, k1.

Row 19: k1, yo, k17, yo, sl1, k2tog, psso, yo, k17, yo, k1.

LEAF MOTIF CHART

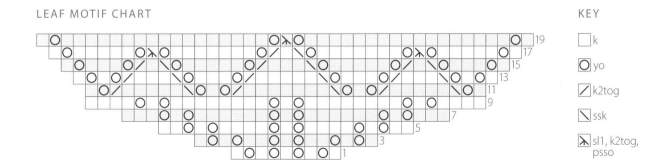

KEY

☐ k

⭕ yo

▧ k2tog

◺ ssk

⋏ sl1, k2tog, psso

CREDITS

Book design:	Julie Levesque www.symposi.com
Tech editing:	Laura Chau www.cosmicpluto.com
Photography:	Rebecca Redston
Production assistant:	Sarah Stanfield

scrumptious

Featuring Scrumptious Yarns from Fyberspates. Distributed in the United States by Lantern Moon.

www.fyberspates.co.uk   www.lanternmoon.com

EBOOK

With a coin carefully scratch off the silver panel opposite to reveal a unique code. To download your complimentary digital version of this book enter the code at:

www.ysolda.com/redeem

COPYRIGHT

Printed and bound in America by Puritan Press on FSC® certified papers using vegetable based inks.
www.puritanpress.com